33716000388381

## DATE DUE

PRINTED IN U.S.A.

BACK
IN
TIME

# LIVING AND WORKING IN
# ANCIENT GREECE

Edited by
Joanne Randolph

**Enslow Publishing**
101 W. 23rd Street
Suite 240
New York, NY 10011
USA
enslow.com

This edition published in 2018 by:
Enslow Publishing, LLC.
101 W. 23rd Street, Suite 240
New York, NY 10011

Additional materials copyright © 2018 by Enslow Publishing, LLC

**Library of Congress Cataloging-in-Publication Date**

Names: Randolph, Joanne, editor.
Title: Living and working in ancient Greece / edited by Joanne Randolph.
Description: New York, NY : Enslow Publishing, [2018] | Series: Back in time
 | Includes bibliographical references and index. | Audience: Grades 3-6.
Identifiers: LCCN 2017001808| ISBN 9780766089716 (library bound book) | ISBN 9780766089693 (pbk. book) | ISBN 9780766089709 (6 pack)
Subjects:  LCSH: Greece—Civilization—To 146 B.C.—Juvenile literature.
Classification: LCC DF77 .L49 2017 | DDC 938—dc23
LC record available at https://lccn.loc.gov/2017001808

Printed in China

**To Our Readers:** We have done our best to make sure all website addresses in this book were active and appropriate when we went to press. However, the author and the publisher have no control over and assume no liability for the material available on those websites or on any websites they may link to. Any comments or suggestions can be sent by e-mail to customerservice@ enslow.com.

**Photos Credits:** Cover, p. 1 Meirion Matthias/Shutterstock.com; series logo, jeedlove/Shutterstock.com; back cover, Reinhold Leitner/Shutterstock.com; hourglass on spine, MilaLiu/Shutterstock.com; pp. 4, 10, 21, 29, 33, 39 Haris vythoulkas/ Shutterstock.com; p. 5 Adisa/Shutterstock.com; pp. 8-9, 22 Universal History Archive/Universal Images Group/Getty Images; pp. 12, 14-15 DEA/G. Dagli Orti/De Agostini/Getty Images; pp. 16-17 DEA/G. Nimatallah/De Agostini/Getty Images; pp. 18-19 Private Collection/Bridgeman Images; p. 25 fritz 16/Shutterstock.com; p. 27 De Agostini/Archivio J. Lange/De Agostini Picture Library/Getty Images; pp. 30, 43 Universal Images Group/Getty Images; p. 32 Swellphotography/Shutterstock.com; p. 34 Print Collector/Hulton Archive/Getty Images; p. 35 Independent Picture Service/Universal Images Group/Getty Images; pp. 36-37 courtesy of The Society for the Revival of the Nemean Games; p. 41 Heritage Images/Hulton Archive/Getty Images.

**Article Credits:** Ann Stalcup, "Land of the Gods," *Faces*; Ann Stalcup, "Welcome to Greece," *Faces*; Angela Murock Hussein, "Meet the Greek Polis," *Dig into History*; John H. Oakley, "School Days," *Dig into History*; Peggy Wilgus Wymore, "Growing Up in Another Time" *AppleSeeds*; R. Anthony Kugler, "Playtime," *Dig into History*; R. Anthony Kugler, "Child Slaves," *Dig into History*; Jane Sutcliffe, "A Trip to the Agora," *AppleSeeds*; "Home Sweet Home," *Dig into History*; Angela Murock Hussein, "Singing in the Shower," *Dig into History*; Karen E. Hong, "It's Greek to Me," *Faces*; Ann Stalcup, "Swifter, Higher, Stronger," *Faces*; Anthony Hollingsworth, "Similarities and Dissimilarities," *Dig into History*; Christine Graf, "Mapping Our World," *AppleSeeds*.

# CONTENTS

# CHAPTER 1

# LAND OF THE GODS

Greece is a land of rugged mountains, shady olive trees, more varieties of wildflowers than any other European country, and islands scattered like jewels across a brilliant blue sea. According to ancient mythology, in a war between the gods, the Titans tore the tops from the mountains, using them as weapons. The rocky peaks fell into the sea, thus creating the many islands of Greece. Mythology, history, and folklore have shaped the way people think in this ancient land; the land itself has shaped their way of life.

You can see the rocky shores rising from the clear, blue waters off the coast of Myrtos Beach, in Kefalonia, Greece. Kefalonia is the largest of the Greek Islands in the Ionian Sea.

# GOVERNMENT THROUGH THE MILLENNIA

Greece is believed to have been first settled around 3000 BCE, when invaders swept down from the north. They failed to reach the island of Crete, home of the Minoans. A literate, advanced civilization with its own hieroglyphic style of writing, the Minoans lived in luxurious cities and palaces. They even had flush toilets, hot and cold running water, and thermal heating. In 1400 BCE, a volcanic eruption on the nearby island of Thera caused earthquakes and tidal waves that destroyed the Minoan civilization. Mainland Greece became the major Mediterranean Sea power.

Around 1200 BCE, the Greeks began forming city-states called poleis. Each had its own rulers, army, and individual type of government. The United States' democracy is based on the style of government Athens had at that time.

The classical period began in the fifth century BCE. Although Greece led the world in science, culture, and the arts, the city-states fought violently among themselves. In 338 BCE, Philip of Macedonia conquered the Greek city-states. His son, Alexander the Great, enlarged the empire, introducing Greek culture to the lands he conquered.

Over the next two thousand years, from 145 BCE onward, Romans, Byzantines, and Ottoman Turks ruled Greece in succession. Although Greece gained its independence from Turkey in 1830, other outsiders invaded Greece. Within the country, there was unrest among the Greeks themselves. Finally, in 1974, Greece rejected its military government and monarchy and became a democratic republic.

# THE LANDSCAPE

Greece is divided into regions and island groups. The landscape, with its barren mountainsides, 9,000-mile-long (14,484 kilometer) coastline, and many islands, has always shaped its people, the way they live, where they live, and the type of work they do. No one lives more than 60 miles (97 km) from the sea. Because of the rugged terrain and dry, rocky soil, agriculture is restricted to one-third of the land. Transportation is difficult. More than nine thousand islands, "flowers of marble," are scattered across three seas—the Mediterranean, Ionian, and Aegean. Only 169 of these islands are inhabited.

Although farmland is limited, Greeks had success growing certain crops, such as olives, figs, raisins, tobacco, and sugar. The bare, rocky land is perfect for growing olive trees.

For centuries, Greeks have been proud of their rich culture and its influence on the peoples of the world, which cannot be measured.

# More on the Greek Polis

Ever notice how often you see the term "city-state" and not "kingdom" or "empire" when reading about ancient Greece? What exactly was this city-state? What made it different from governments in other lands? How was it run and by whom?

## The Name Says It All

During the early first millennium BCE, Greece was a collection of different but separate poleis, each of which had its own urban center, surrounding territory, farmland, and harbor. Most were independent, as Greece was not the unified country it is today.

## Identity Matters

The ancient Greeks did not consider themselves a single people or pledge allegiance to one ruler or one government. Rather, they thought of themselves as citizens of the city-state they called home. Still, they did have much in common, as they shared the same language and worshipped the same gods. They also participated in Panhellenic festivals and athletic contests, such as the Olympic Games.

Today, we think of a city as an urban center within a larger country or state. We see the people and laws of each of these cities as subject to the laws of a particular country and state. The ancient Greek city-state functioned as a small country, with its people subject to the laws and officials of the particular city-state. Each city-state also had its own coinage, looked after its own interests, and often went to war with other city-states, particularly over neighboring territory.

Unlike kingdoms and empires in ancient times, each of which was controlled by an absolute ruler, Greek city-states were governed by their own citizens. In fact, in ancient times, the word *polis* was also used to refer to "the citizen body." For the ancient Greeks, a city-state did not need large buildings in a central location—although many, including Athens—did have such areas. It did, however, need a citizen body to govern it. Each of these citizens had special rights and responsibilities. As a group, citizens elected leaders, drafted and passed laws, held office, and fought their city-states' wars. But, living or being born in a Greek city-state did not automatically grant a person citizenship.

## THE RULES WERE...

In ancient Greece, citizens of a polis had to be freeborn males of a certain age and born to married citizen parents. As most citizens owned land, their fates were closely connected to that of the polis. But what about those who did not qualify for citizenship? According to the laws of the time, wives and children of citizens were not full citizens, but they did have legal rights. Slaves were considered

Athens was the largest, most influential, and most powerful city-state in ancient Greece. It was also the first to develop a democratic form of government, where all its male citizens could vote and take part in government.

property, with very few rights. Ex-slaves, as well as immigrants from other cities or those whose parents were from elsewhere, could never become citizens. The fact that they had lived their entire lives, or most of their lives, in one city-state made no difference.

# CHAPTER 2

# GROWING UP IN ANCIENT GREECE

What was it like to live and grow up in ancient Greece? It certainly was a different world than we are accustomed to today, though some things were similar. Children studied, helped out around the house, and played games. Are you ready to find out more?

# School Days

What was it like to attend school in ancient Greece? What subjects were offered? There is no simple answer to either one of these questions. What you did depended greatly on where you lived and whether you were a boy or a girl. What is certain is that there were no rules governing how long students had to remain in school and no standard curriculum.

We know the most about education in Athens during the period that includes the fifth and fourth centuries BCE. Children stayed at home until they were six or seven years old. Parents, nurses, and slaves played key roles in their upbringing. Then, at six or seven, everything changed. Girls usually remained at home, where older women in a household taught them how to cook, weave, and tend to other domestic chores. Boys, on the other hand, went to primary schools. These were private institutions for which parents paid fees, as there was no free public education in Athens.

# The Three Rs

School started early in the morning and lasted until the afternoon, when students returned home for lunch. Accompanying boys to and from school was their tutor and guardian. Known as the *paidagogos*, he was usually an older slave. Boys often had other teachers as well: the *kitharistes* taught music; the *paidotribes*, physical education; and the *grammatistes*, reading, writing, and arithmetic. The training of the mind and the body were considered equally important in Athens and in much of Greece.

This scene on black figure pottery shows women weaving. Ancient Greek pottery gives scientists insight into what life was like in ancient Greece.

Archaeology preserves considerable evidence of how boys learned to write. First, they memorized the Greek alphabet so that they could recite it backward and forward. Next, they learned to write their names. Once they had mastered these skills, they "graduated" to copying exercises. Initially, they copied lists, then short passages, moving on eventually to long passages. Composition and grammar drills were saved for the more advanced students. The recitation and memorization of works by the great poets, including the *Iliad* and the *Odyssey* by the renowned poet Homer, were considered standard and important exercises. Still intact on surviving fragments of pottery, painted wooden boards, and paper made from the papyrus plant are portions of exercises Greek students completed centuries ago. Many of their writing instruments have also survived. Another source of information about school days are the scenes of boys practicing their writing that have been found on painted Greek vases, as well as scenes that show them playing music, singing, reciting, or involved in sport.

The ancient Greeks considered the lyre the most important instrument. Boys learned to play the lyre as well as to sing to its music. The aulos, a flutelike wind instrument, was also popular at certain times. Around the age of twelve, Greek boys started going to the palaistra. There they learned to run, wrestle, box, jump, and throw the javelin and discus.

# WHEN "CLASS" COUNTS

For most boys, primary school ended when they were fourteen. Only sons of the more prosperous Athenian families continued their education in secondary school, where they studied until the age of eighteen. At that age, boys were required to perform two years of military service for the state. Upon completion, they could continue their education by studying rhetoric or philosophy, often with such renowned academics as the philosopher Socrates (c. 470–399 BCE) and the orator Isocrates (436–338 BCE).

Less privileged boys worked with their fathers learning a trade or helping them in the fields. Girls who were slaves, foreigners, or from the lower classes were sometimes trained to entertain men at the symposium, where they would dance or play music for them.

# A PREFERENCE FOR MILITARY

In Sparta, another major Greek city-state and the archrival of Athens, the educational system was quite different. Sparta's schools were public rather than private. At age six, boys entered the *agoge*, the public educational system. The purpose of the agoge was not to make students men of letters, but rather invincible, loyal soldiers. In many respects, the discipline and training in the agoge were similar to that found in many modern military schools. Spartan girls also received an education. Thus, in the Spartan educational system, the opportunities offered boys and girls were more equitable than elsewhere in ancient Greece.

The city-state of Sparta put a lot more focus on military training than other Greek city-states. This statue shows Leonidas, who was the king of Sparta between 490 and 480 BCE.

# PLAYTIME

With no TV or computer games, what did ancient Greek children do for fun? Lots!

Today scientists and doctors understand the importance of play in a child's development. Games and activities build muscle strength, social skills, and reasoning abilities. The Greeks, too, were firm believers in the benefits of exercise and fitness. They strongly encouraged their children to engage in sports and other physical activities in their spare time. The most common of these were probably footraces, tag, hide-and-seek, and other games that did not require expensive equipment.

While few Greek children would have had more than one or two toys, they managed quite well with what they did have. A single ball, for example, was enough to entertain dozens of children. We do not know much about their ballgames, but many probably resembled modern sports, such as soccer, field hockey, and dodgeball. Passe-boule, the name historians have given to a distinctively Greek game, involved an upright wooden plank with a hole in it. While the rules are not clear to us, the object seems to have been to toss a ball through the hole in the plank to a player or partner on the other side. Both boys and girls played passe-boule, although probably not together.

# GIRLS AT PLAY

While the Greeks tended to emphasize boys' sports over girls' sports, many vase paintings depict girls engaging in a wide variety of recreational activities, including juggling and balancing. Because Greek culture limited opportunities for unmarried girls outside the home, their games, like their education, tended to be less public than their brothers'. This may have worked at times to the girls' advantage, if it allowed them a measure of freedom and creativity that the boys, even in their play, often lacked. Physical play for boys was considered part of their education. As a result, it was monitored closely.

## BONES AS TOYS

Despite the emphasis on physical activities, both boys and girls found time for quieter pastimes. Many of these involved dice, called *astragaloi*, or "knucklebones." Early dice were actually made from the ankle bones of sheep or goats and remained popular even as copies in clay, metal, and other materials became common. Each of the bones used had four distinct sides, and each side was given a numerical value.

This statue from 525 BCE shows a Greek child running. Greek children loved to race, play tag, and play hide-and-seek.

Knucklebones could be used to determine a player's move in a board game or, by themselves, in a variety of betting games. In the latter case, a player generally threw four knucklebones at a time. The best possible outcome was the so-called "throw of Venus," in which each of the four possible values appeared once. The worst was the "Chian throw," named after the island of Chios. In this case, all four bones came up with a value of one. Adults played knucklebones as well, sometimes gambling away large sums of money. Others used them to predict the future. But few adults could match children in their devotion to knucklebones.

# TIMELESS TOYS

Dice are only one of the many small toys that have remained popular from the days of the Greeks to our own time. Tops, marbles, wagons, and clay figurines representing people and animals have all been found in excavations of Greek houses, as have the bones of pets. Greek children were as devoted as we are to birds, dogs, and other animal companions. One popular dog breed kept by ancient Greeks is the now extinct Molossus, used for hunting, herding, and fighting. It is thought to be the ancestor of the modern mastiff.

The playtime needs of children seem to have remained remarkably stable from Greek times to the present. For this reason, games that require only simple, inexpensive toys, or none at all, are an important link to the cultures of the past. The video games of twenty years ago are long forgotten, but the toys of ancient Greece still make children smile.

# CHILD SLAVES

It wasn't fun and games for all children in ancient Greece. Imagine being owned by someone. Imagine having no rights at all. Impossible? Not for these children! Unfortunately, childhood in ancient Greece, as in many parts of the world today, often meant hard physical labor. In many cases, poverty forced parents to assign their own children some of the most difficult household tasks, including carrying water from distant wells. Other children, however, were slaves, whose tasks were assigned not by parents but by owners.

Children became slaves in a variety of ways. While some were simply born into slavery, others were captured in war, kidnapped, or even sold by their parents. The luckiest slaves worked as servants in their masters' households, where loyal service was sometimes rewarded with freedom. The unluckiest worked in the dark and dangerous mines.

Of the few remaining images of child slaves in ancient Greece, almost all depict household workers performing typical chores: carrying wine and serving guests at the parties known as symposia (plural of symposium).

A scene by Makron, the best known of the Greek cup painters, is somewhat unusual in its depiction of a boy exhausted by his serving chores squatting with his head slumped on his shoulders. As a representation of slaves' suffering, Makron's painting is a mild one. A harsher portrayal of slavery and its costs would probably have made the artist's slave-owning customers uncomfortable. It is not surprising, therefore, that the most unfortunate slaves are, artistically and archaeologically speaking, nearly invisible.

# A Trip to the Agora

The agora was the heart of ancient Athens. Part village green, part market, part country fair, the agora was an exciting place. This was where all the important matters of the city-state were discussed and voted upon. It was also a great place to see what some of the jobs in ancient Greece were. Can you picture the scene? People

The Athenian agora was a colorful and busy place.
People came together to share news and shop for goods.

come to hang out with friends and hear the news of the day. They might stop at the barbershop for a haircut. Around the edges of the agora is the bustling marketplace. The narrow streets are crowded with people wearing cloth dyed in shades of red, yellow, green, and bright blue. In the marketplace itself, troupes of jugglers and acrobats keep the shoppers entertained. The calls of the vendors mix with the excited voices of people exchanging the latest gossip. Farmers come to the marketplace to sell their goods, such as sweet figs or ripe, salty olives. A sheep farmer has brought baskets of soft, fluffy fleece. The fishmonger's booth might make you wrinkle your nose. And there's no mistaking the smell of the goat vendor's stall! The craftsmen of Athens show off their wares, too. The jeweler's counter sparkles with gold, silver, and bronze. The sandal maker is always urging people to try on a new pair of sandals. And at the toy seller's are little clay rattles filled with pebbles to keep babies happy. There's really something for everyone here. A hubbub of noise; a spectacle of sights; a carnival of smells, tastes, and textures—this was the ancient agora.

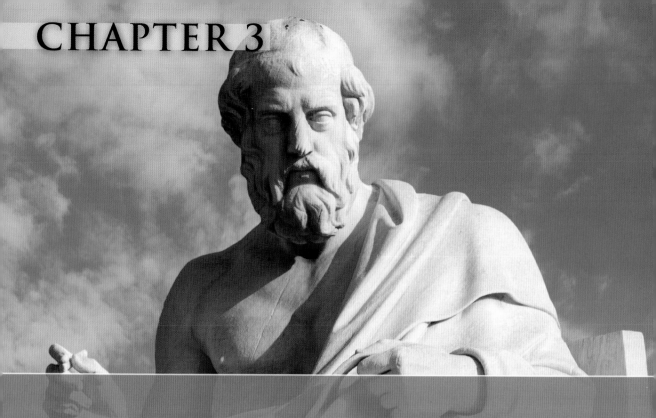

# CHAPTER 3

# HOME SWEET HOME

**W**here do you spend the most time? If you answered "at home," you would be joining the ranks of millions of other people who would give the same answer. Hundreds, even thousands of years ago, the answer again would still most likely be "at home."

So, to understand a civilization and its people, we need to check out its houses. This would be easy in today's world, but travel back in time a few centuries, and the task becomes more difficult. Travel back a few millennia, and it becomes almost impossible.

# A "HOME"LY FIND

Unlike public buildings and palaces, the majority of residential structures are constructed of materials that will shelter a family or families, not for hundreds of years, but for the foreseeable future. Houses are also remodeled, enlarged, or demolished more often than other structures. How then can we learn about life within the home? For scholars and historians, there are two ways: surviving written accounts and artifacts recovered from homes. At Dartmouth College's Hood Museum of Art, re-creation offered a third option, a

This image shows the interior courtyard of an ancient Greek home. There is a status of Hestia, the goddess of the home and hearth.

hands-on approach to finding out what "Home Sweet Home" really meant in fifth-century BCE Greece. To ensure accuracy, the Hood modeled its house on the excavated Dema House.

In the mid-1950s, a discovery was made on the slopes of Mt. Aigaleos to the north of Athens. Fitted stones, mud brick, and other remains suggested that the area had once been the site of a large, rectangular building. Excavation began soon after, and, in 1962, the entire site was uncovered. Among the finds were sections of mud-brick walls, packed-earth flooring, stone door frames, terra-cotta roof tiles, and hard-clay water channels.

# MEETING THE CHALLENGE

Further study indicated that the 72-by-52-foot (22-by-16-meter) structure was a large, freestanding country house from between 425 and 400 BCE. Used only a short time, its end seems to have come abruptly or violently—most likely during the Peloponnesian War (431–404 BCE) between Athens and Sparta. Because the finds show no indication of first-floor bedrooms, the house, known today as the Dema House, must have had a second story.

Before designing the reconstruction, which was called the Friends' House, for the Hood Museum of Art, architect Andrew Garthwaite studied the Dema House site. For Garthwaite, the most challenging part of the project was not re-creating the house, but fitting it into the allotted space within the museum. Two major changes were necessary: no second story and a reversal of room order. The building materials were also different, but the finished model offered visitors the opportunity to experience what "Home Sweet Home" meant in ancient Greece.

# THE FLOOR PLAN

Ancient Greek houses, both in the city and in the country, had a common ground plan. Most were built around a large open courtyard and arranged in a way that allowed as much daylight to enter as possible. Oil lamps of pottery and metal provided additional light. City houses were generally small, consisting of two or three rooms. Those in the country had as many as a dozen rooms. Built of inexpensive materials, such as sun-dried mud bricks stacked on a stone foundation, the houses had plastered or painted walls. Favorite colors were white, red, yellow, and black. The Greeks often decorated their walls with fabric hangings or wall paintings. Most houses had packed-earth or stone floors, but a few were finished with mosaics.

# AT THE BATHS

To the ancient Greeks, the human body was something to be admired. According to them, the outside appearance of an object or person could tell you what it was like on the inside. Attractive people were considered virtuous because the body and soul were connected. Therefore, every Greek aspired to beauty, health, and perfection—a key reason why they enjoyed athletics, since it kept them fit and strong. But another requirement for achieving virtue was keeping clean and well groomed.

In Greece, there were natural streams and brooks that could be used for bathing. However, only those in the country, away from the crowded conditions of the city, were usually clean enough to be usable. The Greeks often used aqueducts to siphon and direct water from the countryside into cities and towns. These aqueducts emptied into large basins in the settlements that were constructed to catch and conserve water. The water was then allowed to flow out through small openings in the basins, creating fountains. These openings were typically carved into the shapes of different animal or human heads. As the water flowed out of the mouths, it looked as if the creatures were spitting. In bathing facilities, the fountainheads were placed high enough up to be used as a shower.

This is part of an ancient Greek aqueduct in Kamares, Greece. The bridge-like structures carried water throughout the city.

# COLD IS GOOD!

But the water in these fountains was not warm. Heating water merely for the purpose of cleansing was expensive, since fuel had to be used for the fire. A warm bath, therefore, was considered very luxurious. Usually, if warm water was used, it was not to fill the tub. Rather, the bather would sit in a small tub and have the water poured over him or her. It was not until Roman times that public bathing facilities with heated water were widely available. Instead, the ancient Greeks believed that cold water was all that was needed to cleanse.

Women and men bathed separately. Women had their own baths or bathed at home. Men's public facilities were more common. There was a small fee to pay for use of the public baths; one ancient Greek inscription mentions an entrance fee of two copper coins, called *chalkoi*.

In bathing facilities, there were always places to hang clothes, either on racks or nearby trees. The Greeks would cleanse their skin with scented oils, the way we use moisturizers and soap today. Popular scents included flowers such as roses and lilies, herbs such as mint and parsley, and spices such as cinnamon and ginger, suspended in olive oil. These aromatic oils would be carried to the bath in *aryballoi*. These small vials with narrow necks had loops of string to place around the wrist or to hang them up while bathing. Skin would not be scrubbed. However, dead skin and dirt would be scraped off with a kind of curved metal implement called a strigil, or scraper. The perfumed oil would be rubbed on the skin before and after scraping.

These ancient remains of a bathhouse are found in Dion, which was part of Macedonia in ancient Greece.

# MEET A "BOOR"

Men's bathing facilities were usually attached to gymnasiums, either in towns and cities or in more rural sanctuaries. In these places, men would gather to work out as well as socialize. Since Greek men often competed in athletics in the nude, they were not modest about bathing together. Of course, some forms of behavior were not considered appropriate while bathing. The fourth-century BCE Greek writer Theophrastus tells us in his book, *The Characters,* that only a person lacking in social graces and culture—a "boor"—would sing in the shower.

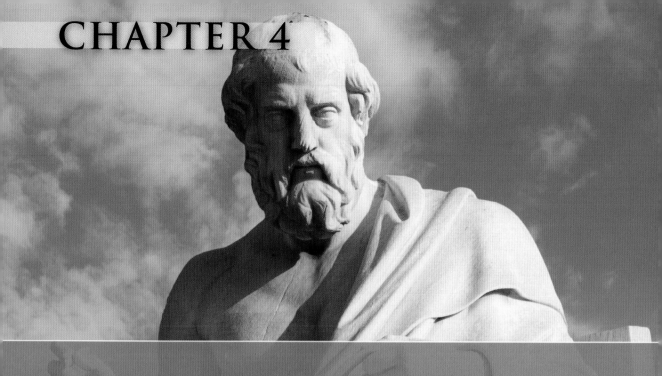

# CHAPTER 4

# LANGUAGE IN ANCIENT GREECE

"It's Greek to me" is often said when something is beyond one's understanding or especially difficult. But nothing could be further from the truth. The Greek alphabet and language look and sound exotic and complicated, but they shaped the vocabulary of Western languages, including English.

When early people began to write, they drew pictures that represented what they were writing about. In about 2000 BCE, early Greeks known as Minoans developed a system of picture or hieroglyphic writing. They used this system to keep accurate records of goods they stored and exported. Their picture writing spread from the island of Crete to mainland Greece.

This disc, called the Phaistos disc, dates from the second millennium BCE. There are hieroglyphic characters engraved in rings on both sides of the disc.

By 1100 BCE, the Greek world was crumbling. As the Greeks abandoned their cities, they forgot about writing. Greece entered a period known as the Dark Ages. No written records survive from this time, and foreign records mention little about the Greeks. But gradually the Greeks prospered and the population grew. They began to trade with the Phoenicians, who lived in present-day Syria.

The Phoenicians developed the first modern alphabet about three thousand years ago. An alphabet is an ordered system of symbols called letters. Each letter represents a specific sound. Because human speech uses about thirty-five different sounds, alphabets need no more than thirty-five letters. Combining letters creates a word. The Phoenician alphabet used twenty-two letters, all consonants.

The Greeks learned the Phoenician alphabet by trading with them. Then Greeks added vowels to the Phoenician alphabet. Vowels represent the breathing between sounds. The English vowels *a, e, i, o,* and *u* grew out of the Greek letters alpha (*a*), epsilon (short *e*), eta (long *e*), iota (*i*), omicron (*o*), upsilon (*u*), and omega (long *o*). Greek became the first alphabet with symbols for both vowels and consonants.

At first, Greek was written from right to left, like the Phoenician alphabet. Later Greek was written in a back and forth style: a line written right to left was followed by a line written left to right. Finally, the writing style shifted again, to left to right, which is how it is still written today.

Although people spoke Greek differently depending on where they lived, the language of Athens, known as Attic, came to be the standard and the language of the great literature of ancient Greece. Attic became the basis for Koine, the common language of the people. When Alexander the Great swept through the Middle East in the fourth century BCE, Koine became the common language of his world. Centuries later, the New Testament of the Bible was written in Koine.

As the centuries passed, Greece became part of the Roman Empire. Although Koine was still spoken by the common people, learned writers turned to an older form of Attic. In the sixth century, classical Greek replaced Latin as the official language of the Byzantine Empire.

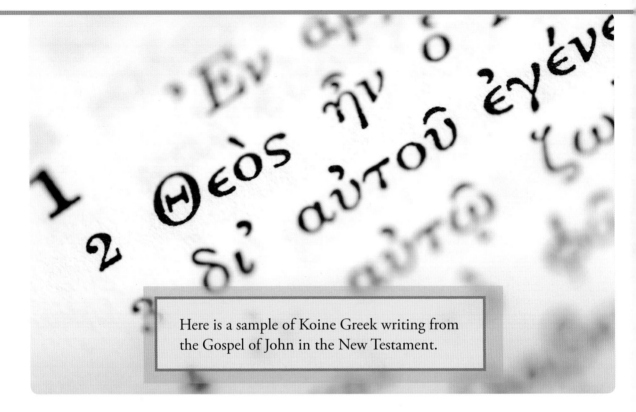

Here is a sample of Koine Greek writing from the Gospel of John in the New Testament.

Modern Greek uses the same alphabet as classical Greek. In 1832, when Greece was recognized as an independent nation, the question of a national language arose. Katharevousa (ka-theh-REV-eh-sa), a compromise between Byzantine and spoken Greek, became the official language from 1834 until 1976. Although Katharevousa is still used in official documents, Demotic Greek, the language used in speech and literature, became the official language of Greece in 1976.

Today, about ten million people speak Greek. Greek words spread from the New Testament and other texts to Latin, German, and English. Greek provides the vocabulary for many arts and sciences. Many English prefixes and suffixes come from Greek. For example, the prefix *psycho-*, as in "psychology," means "the mind" or "mental activity." The suffix *-phone*, as in "telephone," means "sound." With so much Greek in our language, we are right when we say, "It's Greek to me."

# CHAPTER 5

# THE OLYMPIC GAMES

A lthough *Citius, altius, forties* ("Swifter, higher, stronger") is the Latin motto of today's Olympic Games, athletes have been striving to improve their athletic skills since ancient times. All over ancient Greece, athletic contests; dance contests; and horse, boat, and torch races were held. Greek literature describes the many sports that were popular in ancient times; murals and statues show discus throwers, wrestlers, and charioteers.

The Olympic Games were held every four years on the first full moon after the longest day of the year.

Organized games in Greece began 3,500 years ago. By the sixth century BCE, there were several Greek sporting festivals, but the most important one took place in Olympia every fourth summer. The Olympic Games were held in honor of Zeus, the father of the gods. Only citizens of Greek city-states could participate, and the only race, a sprint, was run over a distance called a stade (200 yards or 183 meters). Coroebus, a cook who won the race in 776 BCE, was the first recorded champion.

Gradually, other running events were added, as well as horse racing, wrestling, a pentathlon, chariot racing, and boxing. Athletes competed in the nude; women could neither participate nor watch. At a banquet, champions were presented with olive wreaths.

When Rome conquered Greece in the second century BCE, the games continued. In 394 CE, the Roman emperor Theodosius, a Christian, banned all festivals that honored Olympic gods. The Olympic Games ended. Fifteen hundred years later, in 1887, Frenchman Baron Pierre de Coubertin revived interest in the games.

The modern Olympic Games were organized as a way of promoting peace, friendship, and healthy sporting competition among the youth of the world. Athens, Greece, was chosen as the site of the first modern Olympics. Held in April 1896, the games involved 13 nations, 311 male athletes, 42 events, and 9 sports.

# BASINS AT NEMEA

In Greece, there were four Panhellenic games that were for all Greeks, regardless of which city-state they called home. These were the Olympic Games dedicated to Zeus, the Pythian Games at Delphi in honor of the god Apollo, the Isthmian Games for Poseidon, and the Nemean Games for Zeus and Heracles.

The Pythian Games were held at the stadium in Delphi. You can see the long rows of seats in this photograph of the ruins.

At Nemea, in southern Greece, there was a large temple, as well as several structures used in connection with the games. Among these were a racetrack, lodgings for visitors, and a large bath complex. Dating to the fourth century BCE, the bath is one of the oldest in ancient Greece and definitely the oldest in a Panhellenic sanctuary. An aqueduct made of interlocking clay tiles channeled water from a nearby spring to the complex.

Visitors entered the baths through a large room on the eastern side that was supported by four columns, arranged to form a square. On the wall to the left of the entrance was a door that led to a room on the western side. A row of five columns divided this chamber. To the south of this room was another row of five columns. These lined the bathing area. Through the doorway from the west room, bathers headed down a small set of stairs into a pool that was about chest-deep. On either side of this pool was a smaller room, each with a wall lined with basins at about waist height. Here, bathers could splash or pour water on themselves. The entire bathing room was covered with hydraulic cement and equipped with channels that allowed clean water to enter and wastewater to drain out.

# FOOTRACES

With no starting pistols or lasers, how did the ancient Greeks make sure each runner began a footrace at the same time? Well, the clever Greeks invented an elaborate mechanism called the hysplex. Ancient texts tell us that this starting device consists of two pieces of wood from which cords were stretched, that it was used for both human and horse races, and that it made a loud noise when it was activated. Another clue comes from an ancient inscription in which the names

This is a replica of the hysplex used to start the Olympic Games in ancient Greece. The starters pushed the posts to a vertical position, raising the rope, as runners lined up, then pushed the posts to the ground to drop the rope.

used for individual parts of the hysplex are the same as those used for a catapult.

Excavations at ancient stadiums such as the one at Nemea, where games were held in honor of Zeus every two years, have revealed some interesting holes at the ends of and along the starting line. However, it was only after a Greek vase adorned with figures of runners was found in 1970 that it was finally possible to reconstruct an actual hysplex.

The runners lined up in their respective spaces with their toes inserted into the starting lines. In front of them were stretched two taut ropes attached to two vertical sticks known as elbows. Each "elbow" was set on a small horizontal bar held in place by two cubical blocks, thus allowing it to bend forward like an arm and to bring the ropes to the ground. The elbow was kept upright by a twisted rope that provided torsion like a catapult. When the starter, who stood behind the runners, pulled his rope, he released the barrier, which then snapped to the ground, and all the runners stepped forward simultaneously. Those clever Greeks went to great lengths to make it impossible for runners to cheat in the footrace.

# CHAPTER 6

# IMPORTANT PEOPLE IN ANCIENT GREECE

Three men who lived in ancient Greece shaped philosophy in ways that still affect us today: Socrates, Plato, and Aristotle. Socrates was the first, and his student was Plato. Plato was second, and his student was Aristotle. Aristotle was third, and throughout the ancient world and the Middle Ages, learned men simply called him "the Philosopher."

Each of these men influenced his students, and each helped the other understand how the world works. But each philosopher saw the world differently, especially Plato and Aristotle.

# IDEAL VS. REAL

Plato believed that everything in the world is an image or symbol of something real that we know about but that is impossible to find on earth. That is to say that everything that we see can be compared to pictures of this real object or idea that only exists outside of our world. Thus, a picture of an apple is really only a representation of an actual apple. The same is true, so Plato argued, for everything else in our world. The real entities were called the "forms."

# NOT SO—SAYS ARISTOTLE!

Confusing? Aristotle thought so. In fact, he wrote an entire book called *Categories* just to show everyone that Plato was not exactly right. According to Aristotle, categories, not "Platonic forms," were the answer to defining objects in the world. Aristotle dedicated his life to creating categories, then subdividing them in order to discover the structure of our world. An apple, for example, is a fruit that is red and grows on trees, and so on. Definitions start with very large categories and move into smaller and smaller categories.

# A PAINTING TELLS ALL

One of the best ways to understand the differences between Plato and Aristotle can be found in a picture painted in 1509, almost 1,900 years after they lived. The picture, housed now in the Vatican, was painted by the master Italian Renaissance artist Raphael. Entitled *The School of Athens,* it includes all of the great Greek philosophers.

In *The School of Athens,* Plato and Aristotle are depicted in the center of the fresco, with other influential philosophers surrounding them.

In the very center of the picture, Plato and Aristotle are standing side by side. Plato has his right hand pointing to the sky, while Aristotle has his right hand pointing to the earth. Here was both the similarity and the difference between the two. Both wanted to understand the world, and both saw that there was a structure to the world. Both also looked to the heavens and to earth for answers. But, for Plato, everything on earth was a "mirror image" of the ideal and had to be analyzed as such; Aristotle looked for truth in what he actually saw in the world.

# HAIL TO THE THREE!

Socrates, Plato, and Aristotle changed the way we understand the world, and all three offered compelling views about how the world works. Socrates and Plato seem to have seen the world in much the same way. Plato was a devoted student and honored his teacher by recounting his many conversations. Aristotle, on the other hand, while giving his teacher the respect and honor due to him, still disagreed with him and set out to explain how he believed the world really works.

Ancient Greece produced more philosophers than any other ancient civilization. In fact, ancient Greece is where philosophy began. Thales, the Greeks believed, was the first philosopher. Why? Because he was said to have rejected the idea that the gods controlled everything that happened in nature. He believed that other forces—both mathematical and natural—shaped our world.

# MAPPING OUR WORLD

Greece was not only known for its philosophers. Greece had excellent mathematicians, leaders, and even mapmakers. About forty thousand years ago, the first maps were carved into rock to show the best places to hunt and find nuts and berries. These stone maps also showed the stars and the universe. Of course, rock maps weren't exactly easy to carry around. Eventually, people came up with other ways to make maps. They drew on animal skins, clay, tree bark, cloth, silk, and wax.

# PTOLEMY

More than 1,800 years ago, the world's first great cartographer, or mapmaker, named Claudius Ptolomaeus (Ptolemy), used paper to make his maps. This Greek geographer and astronomer was the first person to put grid lines on a map. These lines, now known as lines of latitude and longitude measure distance north, south, east, and west and make it easier to locate places on a map.

Merchant travelers shared their maps and charts with Ptolemy. Ptolemy wrote books that explained mapmaking, or cartography, and contained a world map and maps of Europe, Africa, and Asia, which included the coordinates for eight thousand cities, rivers, and mountain ranges around the world.

Ptolemy's maps were made and used during a time when the Greeks

Ptolemy holds an armillary sphere, which shows the position of bodies in space. Ptolemy's sphere shows Earth in the center. Later spheres would show the sun in the center.

and Romans ruled much of western Europe and the Mediterranean world. When the Christian church gained power around the year 400, the church replaced Ptolemy's maps with new maps that were based more on religion than on actual geography. The church's maps showed east at the top of the map because that is where the biblical Garden of Eden was believed to be. These Christian maps always included a picture of Jesus and showed the holy city of Jerusalem at the center of the world.

Then, in the 1400s, Ptolemy's maps resurfaced in Europe. European explorers, including Christopher Columbus, used them to navigate around the world. About the same time, the printing press was invented. This made maps more common and more accessible. Historians call the 1400s and 1500s the Age of Exploration. Explorers went out from Europe around the globe trying to discover new lands. They brought back information that allowed mapmakers to make better maps. They discovered that Earth was quite a bit larger than Ptolemy had thought. They also realized that he had made Asia too big and that he left out a few details—the Americas, Australia, and the Pacific Ocean, for example.

# LASTING INFLUENCE

From philosophy, government, art, and architecture to mathematics, theater, and more, the ancient Greek legacy lives on in today's society. All of Western civilization stands on the foundations built by the Greeks in so many areas. Thank you, ancient Greece!

# CHRONOLOGY

**c. 2000 BCE** A group of people called the Hellenes moves into the area now called Greece.

**c. 1200 BCE** After ten years of battle, Greece defeats Troy in the Trojan War.

**776 BCE** The first Olympic Games are held.

**c. 750–500 BCE** Greek city-states, each with a polis as its center, develop along the coastal areas of the Mediterranean and Black seas.

**490 BCE** Persia invades Greece but is defeated in the Battle of Marathon. Persia tries again to gain control of Greece but is beaten a second time.

**475–400 BCE** Greece experiences its golden age. Many ideas about philosophy, mathematics, architecture, and literature that developed at this time still influence the modern world.

**431–404 BCE** Athens and Sparta square off in the Peloponnesian War. Athens and many other city-states begin to diminish in power.

**336 BCE** Alexander the Great, a student of Greek teacher Aristotle, proclaims himself commander in chief of all Greece and spreads Greek culture to the many lands he conquers. At the time of his death, Alexander's empire includes parts of Europe, Africa, and Asia.

**146 BCE–330 CE** Greece is part of the Roman Empire.

**331–1453** The Eastern Roman Empire, called the Byzantine Empire, controls Greece.

**1453–1821** Greece is under control of the Ottoman Turks.

**1821** March 25 is Greek Independence Day.

# GLOSSARY

**aqueduct**  A bridge created to carry water.

**cartographer**  A mapmaker.

**citizen**  A legally recognized subject of a nation or commonwealth, especially one entitled to its privileges, such as the right to vote.

**city-state**  An independent city that has its own government and is separate from other countries.

**civilization**  The society, culture, and way of life of a particular area.

**democracy**  A system of government by the people or the eligible members.

**hieroglyphic**  Writing that is pictographic, or where characters resemble pictures.

**latitude**  A geographic coordinate that tells the north-south position of a point on Earth's surface.

**literate**  Able to read and write.

**longitude**  A geographic coordinate that tells the east-west position of a point on Earth's surface.

**lyre**  A small U-shaped harp.

**philosophy**  The study of the nature of knowledge, reality, and existence.

**rhetoric**  The art of effective and persuasive speaking or writing.

# FURTHER READING

## BOOKS

Nardo, Don. *Life in Ancient Greece*. San Diego, CA: ReferencePoint Press, 2015.

O'Brian, Pliny. *Myths of Ancient Greeks*. New York, NY: Cavendish Square Publishing, 2016.

Pearson, Anne. *Ancient Greece*. London, UK: DK Eyewitness Books, 2014.

Roscoe, Kelly, and Mick Isle. *Aristotle: The Father of Logic.* New York, NY: Rosen Young Adult, 2015.

Wilhelm, Doug. *Alexander the Great.* New York, NY: Children's Press/Franklin Watts Trade, 2015.

## WEBSITES

**The British Museum**
*www.ancientgreece.co.uk/gods/home_set.html*
Learn about the ancient Greek gods and goddesses.

**National Geographic Kids**
*www.ngkids.co.uk/history/10-facts-about-the-ancient-greeks*
Read ten fascinating facts about ancient Greece.

**UShistory.org, Ancient Civilizations**
*www.ushistory.org/civ/5.asp*
Dive deeper into the history and culture of ancient Greece.

# INDEX